Welcome

It's easy to forget how important it is to take time for yourself amid the chaos and stresses of everyday life. Getting creative is a great way to unwind and colouring is the perfect outlet for those who want to relax in the comfort of their own home. This colouring book is jam-packed with outrageously adorable kitties that will help you find a moment of peace in your hectic day. So, whether you want to take a step into the world of mindfulness, or you just want to explore your creative side, grab your colouring pencils and bring these cute critters to life!

FUTURE

LET'S COLOUR
Cute Cats

Future PLC Quay House, The Ambury, Bath, BA1 1UA

Editorial
Group Editor **Philippa Grafton**
Art Editor **Madelene King**
Head of Art & Design **Greg Whitaker**
Editorial Director **Jon White**
Managing Director **Grainne McKenna**

All images
Getty Images, Shutterstock

Advertising
Media packs are available on request
Commercial Director **Clare Dove**

International
Head of Print Licensing **Rachel Shaw**
licensing@futurenet.com
www.futurecontenthub.com

Circulation
Head of Newstrade **Tim Mathers**

Production
Head of Production **Mark Constance**
Production Project Manager **Matthew Eglinton**
Advertising Production Manager **Joanne Crosby**
Digital Editions Controller **Jason Hudson**
Production Managers **Keely Miller, Nola Cokely,
Vivienne Calvert, Fran Twentyman**

Printed in the UK

Distributed by Marketforce – www.marketforce.co.uk
For enquiries, please email: mfcommunications@futurenet.com

Let's Colour Cute Cats First Edition (CTB6111)
© 2024 Future Publishing Limited

Future plc is a public
company quoted on the
London Stock Exchange
(symbol: FUTR)
www.futureplc.com

Chief Executive Officer **Jon Steinberg**
Non-Executive Chairman **Richard Huntingford**
Chief Financial and Strategy Officer **Penny Ladkin-Brand**

Tel +44 (0)1225 442 244

13

17

21

34

35

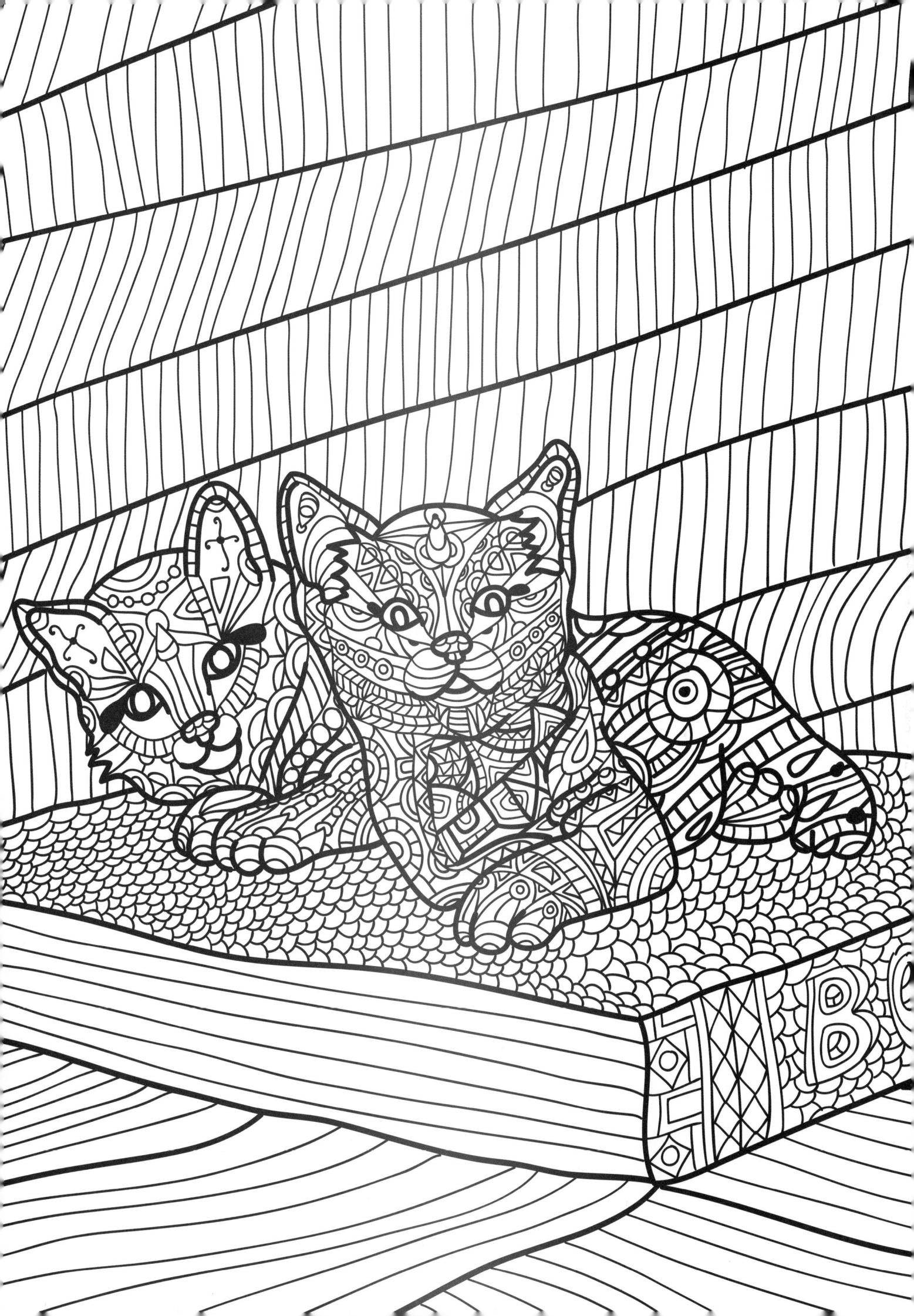

44

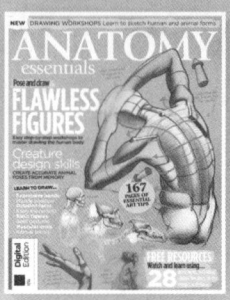
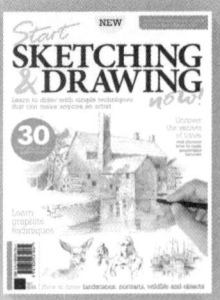